# CUTE CRITTERS
## AT CHRISTMAS

Cute Critters having fun in the sun, snow, and anywhere they want to go!
They're wrapping presents, making gingerbread, and getting ready for the holidays.
Come join the fun and help them bring some of their favorite traditions to life!

PUBLISHED IN 2024 BY STOP N' SMILE PUBLISHING

# CUTE CRITTERS TO COLOR!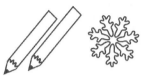

In modern times stress is at an all time high. Coloring is a way to melt that anxiety away, one page at a time. At Stop n' Smile publishing, we want you do to precisely that - take a second to stop with intention and be happy.

## WHAT'S THE NARWAL DOING?

Enjoy Alluring Alliterations from Cute Critters as they journey through the Holiday Season. Suspend belief for a few whimsical pages, and delight in everything from Dogs Decorating Trees to Yaks Yodeling!

## WORK ZONE!!

While you're working so are we! Each page has been uniquely crafted and is waiting for a coloring artist like you to bring it to its merry life. If you have any recommendations for future places or scenarios you'd like to see Cute Critters in, please reach out!

## CONTACT US:

If you have any feedback, we are always trying to make out books better.
Feel free to reach out :
*contact.stopnsmile@gmail.com*

# BEFORE YOU BEGIN...

As you start coloring you will probably notice that the standard
page material from Amazon is not very thick.
It is ideal for crayons and pencils, but will likely bleed through
if you use wet materials like markers or paints.

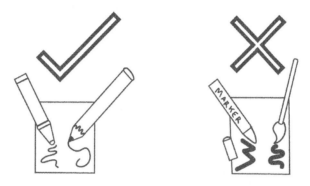

We understand you may still want to use those materials,
in which case we recommend either putting a piece of paper between pages
as you work, or cutting that page out of the book.

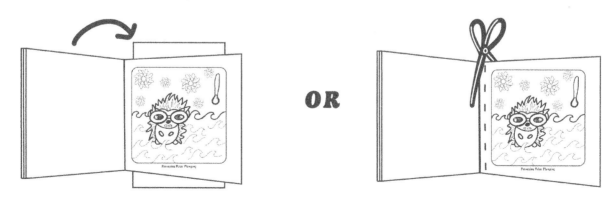

OR

Snowflakes come in all shapes and sizes!

Try drawing your own!

An Alligator Opening An Advent Calendar

Bison Builiding Snowmen

Camels Caroling

Dogs Decorating

Elephant Making Eggnog

Frog Family Gift Exchange

Giraffe Decrorating Gingerbread

Hippopotamus Hanging Stockings

Iguana Ice Fishing

Jellyfish Jamming To Jingle Bells

Kangaroo Knitting Christmas Sweaters

Lions Looking at Lights

Monkeys Under Mistletoe

Narwhal Nordic Skiing

Owl Organizing Ornaments

Porcupine Polar Plunging

Quail Quilting

Raccoon Roasting Chestnuts

Seahorse Sledding

Turtles Trumpeting

Urchin in an Ugly Christmas Sweater

Vulture Visiting Santa

Walrus Wrapping Presents

Xerus Xmas Cookie Making

Yak Yodeling

Zebra Ziplining